ALSO BY DANIELE PANTANO

Translations

The Possible Is Monstrous: Selected Poems by Friedrich Dürrenmatt (2010)
In an Abandoned Room: Selected Poems by Georg Trakl (2008)

THE OLDEST HANDS IN THE WORLD

THE OLDEST HANDS
IN THE WORLD

Poems

Daniele Pantano

Black Lawrence Press
New York

Black Lawrence Press
www.blacklawrence.com

Executive Editor: Diane Goettel
Book Design: Steven Seighman

Black Lawrence Press
115 Center Ave.
Aspinwall, PA 15215
U.S.A.

Author photo © Nicole R. Pantano
Cover photo © Matt Lewis

Published 2010 by Black Lawrence Press, a division of Dzanc Books

First edition 2010
ISBN: 978-09826318-6-7

Printed in the United States

For Fiona and Giacomo—*You are what I cannot write*

Tu non sai le colline dove si è sparso il sangue.
You do not know the hills where the blood flowed.

—Cesare Pavese

CONTENTS

THE OLDEST HANDS IN THE WORLD

I.

LAST VISIT & SUPPER PRIOR TO THE INVASION
ONLY WE KNEW ABOUT

Finally. Dessert. He opened
The shutters and revealed
Everything that would cease
To matter the next day. Alleys
Where men were playing another
Round of chess—accents equally
On time and women parading
Like citrus trees in a market of dates.
Pubs. Songs. Palaces of worship.
No. Not even the orphanage
Or his pregnant wife's glutted breasts
Would matter. My host insisted
I spend my time writing the important,
Not the beautiful. *What else can we do?*
He asked. *Continue*, I answered.
And excused myself. All of it.
Except my uncleared plate:
Lemon wheels and spilled milk.

II.

BETWEEN STATIONS OF THE METRO

How wonderfully it all matches the black bough:
Her artificial leg she sways as flesh. Fingers forking
His beard and the thinning images he considers.
A boy's grin held by two cheeks. Fists. Simple
And unprovoked, like our apparitions we share
Each morning, *en passant*, from crests of departure
To whatever we still believe possible. How silly.
How silly to think we all reemerge as petals—pulled
Loose. Bereft of what kept us from the rain.

THÉÂTRE DU GRAND GUIGNOL

Fifty lifeless characters animated.

The audience, astonished, reflects upon the preeminent importance:
A curtain that never falls.

Performance and terror often contain an unconscious existence.

Vacuous eyes

Nonchalantly rising above any great and definite achievement,
While the Playbill attends a memorable ceremony:

A writer's death flanked by language.

The stage conceives a stranger, a sage, matters of occultism,
In an attempt to stimulate man's inner need
To move toward an addressable reality.

But the audience still believes in imitation, nothing more . . .

The applause raucous.

THE OLDEST HANDS IN THE WORLD

On this chair, as I am every morning, waiting
For the cappuccino and brioche to arrive,

And the girl with the oldest hands in the world,
I sense exile is a city reared by eternal artifice.

All sweet violence and thought and repetition.

Beyond what history has left of this topography,
The cup is whiteness, the coffee brown semen.

My first sip makes her appear with provender
And sandals from behind the insignificant ruins.

But for the time being, ruins are eucalyptus trees.
And she not a girl on her way to feed chickens

But a face concealed by dripping nets. Dressed
In black sails and hair dyed a Roman blonde.

The lips of her soul are burning sages, I know.
Her name, I don't. Only her hands matter.

Laden with broached scars, they remind me—
Home is where children sprout in rippled soil.

Where footsteps are mosaics of possibility.

To go on. Finish breakfast. Read the line
That ends in God's breath. Again.

CICADAS IN THE VALLEY OF TEMPLES

for L. Pirandello

Offer the Akragantine men an origin of movement
A nexus with the glorious temples that filter modernity

STREETS THAT END IN YOUR NAME

A city will not remember your name unless you find it in her streets.

But youth unearths its names as pages torn
From a banned text: a scrapbook of stains.

We cannot allow this city to ignore us.

We piss our names on the walls of cathedrals.
Watch how letters seep through history.

When the night seizes its wounds, no one is a stranger.

Beneath the onerous arch, we scorch
Our maps. Sow ashes for the Lost.

Everything is real; nothing can be stolen.

Our legless voices snap an unknown line.
A bough broken across worn doorways.

Have you been hurt? Come and take a close look.

Climb the highest walls. Sit. Drink another
Bottle. Toss it. See it fall. Howl as it shatters.

EROSION

When the crisis of the sea declares her anger, the island women
Fasten their clotheslines. Hang used panties for the wind to carry
Their scent across the triangular land. And as the sea's spontaneous
Capitulation adjourns another conquest, the men in the mountains thank
Their saints for fertile land and curse the women for their wretched games.

CONVERSATIONS NEAR SAN PIERO PATTI, SICILY

As for the farmer, he talks about American soldiers
With pedigreed hands who met him on the outskirts
To trade cigarettes for wine and tomatoes—the land
Scorched by poverty they had heard so much about
Back on Mulberry Street. While the British, skidding
Past on motorcycles, heading into town, abandoned
Their promises once the tomatoes were eaten
And the bottles of wine emptied.

7 JULY 2005 (NOTE FOUND ON
A LONDON SUBWAY CARRIAGE)

What I enjoy about chaos is the guarantee of creation
The rapid unexpected

VALKYRIE THIGHS

Everything becomes nuclear.
Crystallized. Faceted. The impact

Catapults me out of the seat
And onto a mountain of Valkyrie thighs.

I'm home again. In the distance
Ravens feast on schoolbooks and suburban

Girls. They cannot run anymore.
Listen to the old house speak to its insolent dogs.

Here, restrictions are incomprehensible.
Notebooks are currency. Who can say
The least earns the newest fashions.

We eat tomatoes before they are green.

AND THE CORRESPONDENCE AMONG
   OURSELVES

Remains anonymous. We are not bothered by faces. We are
Not bothered by the smell of oranges. Only the reserved fit
Of frames. Ghosts who disregard our soul's varnished wood.
Who rest within. Inflict tender periods of madness and exit.
Only to return unannounced. Over. And over. And over.

SPADAFORA

Upon crossing the crowded promenade of this fishing village,
One experiences the metamorphosis of a neighborhood—

With its colonies of wild, black-haired women, its faded
Architecture gutted by salt, its voices shepherded by wine

And lava, its parameter stretching towards mountain orchards,
And its aroma of religious perspiration, infernal passion,

And ancient gastronomy—by blessing the dormant boats
And pushing the sun along the dynamics of the sea.

THE STRANGER

I saw her in the mirror of the burnt hall
Her black hair spreading across Europe

EVERY MOMENT OCCURS AFTER
A SEQUENCE OF LOOKS

1.

Anticipate the whipping beauty of these southern women
Accustomed to euphoria within the word.

2.

Inform them that they're unable to solicit the final embalming.

3.

Language consists of minute fractures near each climax.

4.

Confirm the impossible: to fully comprehend any experience.

5.

We can die at once and laugh about it.

6.

Proclaim days are dominated by sex, verbs, red paint.

7.

Witness the death of a praying mantis as her black hair finally settles.

III.

FALLEN

My grape harvest appeared meaningless.
Until, among the vineyard's decay, I found
Her skin. Her mind. November's gelid veins.

I knew my thirst. So I crushed her body
With the phallic weight of August—trousers
Unbuttoned, skirts raised by gypsy hymns—
To douse my lips with her caustic sap.

Every grape reveals a different poison.
Every woman stems from a different grape.

VENETIAN DUET

We step onto the narrow bridge. She lifts her skirt. Summons me
To play her succulent violin. Draw my tongue across black strings.
Compose the sonata of a million unborn sins. Nocturnes circulate
As evening sighs the adagio of executions.

LA HORA CERO:
ESCHATOLOGICAL FRAGMENTS

after Astor Piazzolla

(Death—Tango)

You can hear us.
   Through the walls.

Tango, tragedia,
   Comedia, kilombo.
Tango, tragedia,
   Comedia, kilombo.

The Whore, I.
   The maggot feeding.
On her blood.
   Her scent, my flesh.
Prodding her misery.

(Judgment—Tragedia)

   At this hour.
Memory is she.
   Who shouts *ganchos.*

The moment.
   As language.

One step further.
   To receive.

(Heaven—Comedia)

We are both.
   Sides of morning.

Appease the horizon.
  With a crowning descent.

  (Hell—Kilombo)

Suffering erotic convulsions.
  We devour thighs.
And draw circles.
  In the half-light.

Illuminating our dance.
  Our magic identification.

FUGUE

Night harvests her scent. Unfurled limbs: the calligraphy of seduction.
Nomads whisper sixty-nine borders. Dermal concord. Each crossing
A pant of energy. Each penetration a lacuna of refuge.

LULLABY

Through my window.
Myths of grapes. Cacti.

Burning fuel. I notice
My daughter's slumberous

Smile. Cough heavily
Across waters. Flames

Rise to devour a hill
Amidst the Sicilian night.

WITH FIONA, AGE 2, IN THE GARDEN

You enjoy no equals in the infinite world of perception.
Recognize the root of an appearance.

Advance with confidence and ease. Respond to it
As you turn to behold my ignorant gaze.

Know that your glances assemble my reunion
With the essence of existence.

My retreat from time and knowledge: science
Of life's bastard progenies.

PATRIMONIAL RECIPE

I swore never to wear my father's mask.

Yet I meticulously peel and cut tomatoes.
Crush garlic. Pluck basil bent
Low in observance. One
By one. Push them off the plank.

Into the fervid blonde of olive oil.

Salt. Pepper. Dash of sugar.
Then I sit down at the table.
Yell at my children for being children.
Ignore my wife—her voice:

The steam of boiling water.

And wait for the perfect consistency.
Al dente. The callous core that weeps

When overcooked.

WITNESS

Realize the inability to emulate the basic pattern. Hear the blatant
Silence of dynamos. Feel the will's sudden sting. Moments carved
In transient silhouettes veil the evening's restless minds. A stroll
Towards a dark room captures the image of bloodshot eyes, smiling
At the young mother and her gun.

EINE KLEINE NACHTMUSIK

My infant son is the moon.
His face with the crescent smile.

Sleep's music renders us equal.

Soon, we shall dance in the morning
Forest of olive trees.

EASTERN VILLAGE WITH FACTORY

Dogs bark in untended fields. Outside, artificial light
Pools the road nobody's died on with men sauntering
The graveyard shift, unafraid to sing alone. I stretch out
And find I married a woman who doesn't care that they
Have picked up the ambrosial bouquet of sex—neatly
Wrapped in tissue paper—at the foot of our bed. She
Welcomes the rabid charge. Anything that reminds her
She belongs to the faint hinterland. She keeps the doors
Unlocked. I say nothing. Men or dogs. There will be no
Other end.

TIME

Their last embrace

To conserve this moment
He imagines time
As a kaleidoscope of lovers

Every artless turn a new possibility

*

As a circle

Every embrace infinite in its repetition
Eternal recurrence of immutable gestures

One can let go—and simply wait . . .

*

Is discontinuous

Glimpses of the sometime / the impending / the steps of travelers
The first taste of lemon ice / the numbness of hands

Every embrace a filament of light

*

Without quality

His grasp resembles a dying child
Lovers never leave

Intensity dictates the duration of every touch

*

As reflection

Ballistics, propelled emotions

(mirrors populate the panorama—all is shared a thousandfold)

Every departure a bulwark of pain

*

Without memory

She fades into the pulse of foreign scriptures
As his eyes scan pages for the familiar

Every good-bye is death

*

World without Time

Still life of a final kiss

*

As woman

Gently her arms wrench away to a future past
Their first fuck, their first encounter

The day her eyes will mean nothing to him

DOPPELGÄNGER

Back. At the Luxembourg. People watching. For you. I will
Not cleave to the cardinal semblance. Passing the odd-shaped
Lake. Flagging. The remains. After all this time. We mistake
For our past. The smolder of '68 Citröens. Our adulterous
Riots. In these beds of flowering tobacco. *There is no absence*
That cannot be replaced. Your favorite line. I rose against. Today.

SUDDEN DISAPPEARANCE

Q:

Is it enough that his family will never know
What happened to him? That he did not
Remember my face as I approached, as he saw
My eyes lose color? Is it enough that I tied
His legs, taped shut his mouth . . . that he begged
When I revealed the knife? Is it enough that I
Repeated my mother's name as I slowly slit his
Throat? That the cut gave him ample time to rest
His head on the spare tire, to wait, to bleed? Is it
Enough that I closed the trunk? That my final blow
Could be heard for the rest of that late spring?

A:

The prime cause renders justice a possibility, a possibility
That vanishes with its purest execution.

MOVING

Leaving the house
Whose cracks mimic

My own, I forsake
An insensible history.

Only one life
Can be boxed.

Laughter and terror
Ingrained in wood floors,

The other abides with impressions
Of what cannot be carried.

IV.

TRAKL'S SEASON

Every image secretes its most haunting confessions. How to
Distinguish between voice and breeze in this lonely season—
Trace the maple's grief or follow blackbirds' lament into spring?

....

With frigid hands brushing against burning poppy fields. A seat.
Reverie of decaying laughter from soldiers with shattered mouths.

....

The wait for a stranger's lost shadow to muddle this autumnal foliage
That greets ancient pilgrims, whose voices once rested here to join
The discussions of drowned children.

....

How to distinguish between voice and breeze in this lonely season?

AMERIKA

after Modigliani

Parked by the ocean, I can still hear you
In the first syllables of my new language.
Always keep the directions that brought you here.
Foolish me, after a few days, I shredded
The map I knew like the lining of my pockets.

....

What I wouldn't give for one quick glance
At those directions—anew, inverted—body
As knowledge, knowledge as body. You offer
Everything I've lost, but with this new tongue,
Hesitant to taste even the most familiar, I
No longer speak. In a language not mine, in all
New languages, all words spell "forgetting."

....

I'm left with years of white pages.

....

Oh, but a painter's imagination keeps me
From surrendering, drives me back passed
Your acned skin, scarred streets, passed nipples
Of industry, your terrorized sex. And I will drive,
Drive until I know your soul, until I can paint
Your eyes: two maps . . . one for each pocket.

SIMIC'S ARMY OF SPIDERS

He orders them to his New Hampshire basement. It is 1990.

He gives no reasons. Only the promise to entertain with moths
And fireflies made from nails, aluminum foil, wire. Quickly

The spiders realize poetry's offal doesn't suit dainty stomachs.
And march to stage their gossamer putsch. Head thrown back.

Eyes trampled raw. Stringing sentences on a neck of war. Simic bleeds
In his study. Hears them hail his lesion. Knot arachnid snares. Chart

Untold festivals in honor of the coup d'état. A wounded prey, he shares
Their vision. To spin a web of names. Trap something so immense.

Its every pore—a country of light.

CHESS AT NIGHT (BACKYARD, FLORIDA)

Out here. Any given opening. An immediate surrender.
A deliverance into blades of grass. Hammered too sharp.
Too violent by a game life can no longer stage. So what?
When once or twice you see someone turn on the lights
In the old nursery? Your opponent's missing army?

BEYOND THE STOP SIGN: SWISS LANDSCAPE

Fictitious. This green. Like no other. This blue. Conscious.
Spectators. We agree. Language at birth. The rush. At once.
Forever. Scourged by origins and locutions. We find ourselves.
Back to it. The octagon. Its base. Like a senate of fatidic ants.
Ready. For the scouts. To move. From red. To white. To red.

IN AN ABANDONED WAREHOUSE

for F. Wright

Philosophy failed!

The banner no one could read pronounced.

WRITING THE CITY

I fail the city I left because its voices
Failed me. Writing hours for nothing
But a second, I thought they would
Come easy after more than a decade.
The voices that silenced mine.

....

Not the baker's murmur as he opens
Shop at 4 a.m. Nor the garbage men's
Clatter. My brother cussing somewhere
Climbing scaffoldings to paint another
House he'll never own. My father's song
Sanding my name knifed into the door
I slammed a thousand times. School-
Children dropping books to reach fruit
The way I did. It's the teachers, principals,
Officials, and all who refused my immigrant's
Voice born among them.

....

The Swiss city I left can never be written.
Perhaps the windows, shutters, each beautiful
Roof with rain. The medieval intimacy of space
Against the omnipotent alps. My voice finds
Itself in every detail of this—until it confronts
What can never be said.

GUINEA PIGS

Having accused—executed—bled—skinned—scattered them
For the beasts of Schoren Forest—we shot down the hillside
On a black sled. Scared shitless—my brother—clutching
My boyish waist—knees bent—nose against ribs—not
Because of what we'd done—speed—or father's finger-splitting
Belt—but because he'd forgotten his smile as the creatures' bodies
Went as cold and flat as Grandpa's blades used to slaughter *Schweine.*
December never ended without it—them—hung like pink whales
In a heavy sky—blood-soaked hay—fires readied—ground littered
With hooves. And whenever mother lugged another fatback inside—
Großvater—gutting—would say: *Remember—don't be taking unless you're giving—*
Smile when you kill—He'll remember when it's your turn. Later—led
By mother's suicide note—I hit upon those meats—tucked away—
An overcured history of infidelities—marriages—abortions—a box
Of Walker's Pure Butter Shortbread Petticoat Tails filled with *Wehrpaß*—
Battle Map—Iron Cross—Photos: Grandpa smiling—(striking, in
uniform)—(Strained, in Leningrad)—(deadly, between my freshly slit
fingers).

CHILDHOOD SEX AND VIOLENCE
(FOUR SCENES)

FADE IN:

EXT. SUMMER   AFTERNOON

Hide and seek. Hours
In my favorite hiding spot:
The communal bathroom—
My personal Sistine Chapel
With one stall and interminable
Spreads of frescoes—where I
Encounter poetry, sitting stock-
Still, gripped by color and ink:
Brick portraits of dripping cunts
And spitting cocks and tits and

Call me! I'll suck you dry and eat your shit.

Golden showers? I'm here on Mondays and Fridays.

Cum all over me!

Those votive offerings beckon me
Away from wog hunting kids
To stay and create.

               SELF (V. O.)
Ready or not, here I come.

INT. FALL   NIGHT

Remodeling. My four walls turn
Into a makeshift living room.
Father's there for three months,
Watching TV on the couch.
He jerks off while I pretend
To sleep. Thinking of what
To wear for school the next day,
I hear him wash his hands
In the half-finished bathroom.

INT. WINTER   MORNING

I begin dealing pornographic
Tapes in fifth grade. The money:
Classmates, their parents, grand-
Parents. Academic progress:
Nonexistent, except for the study
Of mother's rented rooms
With Albanian and Serbian men,
For which no marks are offered.

EXT. SPRING   EVENING

I feel alive running with mountain
Beasts and giants, churning the sky
With William Tell's hissing bolts.

                              FADE OUT

VISIT AFTER A MISSED REVOLUTION

You cannot see the famous writer. The police
Relocated him and kissed him good-bye. One
Of them kept on saying, *tell us about it . . . tell us*
About it. What do you do? I thought we might all be
Of that something . . . .

SPEEDOMETER NEEDLE

Foot anchored, its head lashes past lit auguries.
Governed by eyes firm to embrace, to forge
A carbon fiber skirt around the nearest tree,
Its slash body, mounted by g-forces, succumbs
To an impetuous grin: acceleration's blackout.

Hood furrowed / Chassis rived / Headlights Craned.

Man's invention which most resembles a living thing
Bears the same fatal flicker as our suicidal tongues
Anticipating the metallic savor of a .40 caliber cock.

V.

MORNING WALK

for J. Hopler

Today, let me not ponder life or love or
Who fans the flame at the center of all things

Today, let me simply accept the bombinating
Presence of death in everything I see

EVERY SO OFTEN

Remembrance appears
As a reminder: nothing

In our lives disappears.
It all merely lingers—
Faceless, here and there.

And every so often
It knocks on your door
Seeking shelter for the night.

THE AXIOLOGY OF TASTE

I return as a man to the kitchen
Where I was taught the difference
Between cardamom and cinnamon.

I make a dish out of nothing.

Father says I still use too much salt.

WHEN SIGHT BECOMES UNBEARABLE,
SPRING 1945

1.

Miles outside the camp, the very last cattle car
Stood yet to be discovered.

2.

In it, men, women, and children, who had torn each other's eyes out.

3.

Sat with open wrists, listening—

4.

Blood drying as tears on unblemished skin.

5.

Barred shafts of light unhinging a heart-
Beat. Its decrescendo to the coda's final note:

6.

When sight becomes unbearable.

7.

The voice of darkness is the hope in every mother's womb.

WOOD OF SUICIDES

Drop this soil sodden with torment
Before the scalpel rain peels your twined fist.

Drop it. By the thicket where you kissed children,
Dug your fingers into the dirt, buried them without prayer.

Drop it. Mark the causality of forgiveness, of sin,
Alongside river Phlegethon's seething maelstrom,

Its spiral narrative. Your barked soul that shelters your scars.

ESCAPE ARTIST

My mother missed her own funeral.

Why or how she did it is a mystery.
Or a fantasy. I barely remember.

The blow of absence that shut the priest's
Voice like a child's very first nightmare.

The lump of air in my throat I kneaded
Until it became smoke, became breath.

Language, nestled up against silence.

A lunatic sashaying past, grinning,
Doesn't anyone know where she is?

What can I say? We all missed it. And left.

Well, no wonder, someone muttered
On my way past the holy water,
She's a suicide, you know . . . and a whore.

Yes, I thought.
Not even God can create a net without holes.

4:36 AM

for G. Smith

The poet who forgets to eat when his lovers are away
Sits up in bed and instantly tears off his skin
To exploit raw, secure motion—turns

Fondles her with dangling nerves

Pardon me, you mind a drink?
Naturellement, the Word says.

(a few pubic hairs sticking
to the bottom of her tongue).

Le Pont Mirabeau is never far.

He fucks with injurious vision.

MOUNTAIN LIFE

One northern night the perfect poem will arrive.
I will type it, read it once, and throw it away.

Gulp my aquavit. Take my cigarettes. Very gently
Kiss my kids. And her. Put on my wool cardigan.

Walk to the fjord and stay for the first ferry,
Reckoning how not to write the subsequent life.

NOTEBOOK ENTRIES (NINE YEARS AFTER HER DEATH)

1

Foreign Policy

The attractive American requested the uncommon after the traditional Production. The native theatre erupted with laughter. In response she Rose to pierce the gallery of blood oranges with her Italian-made stiletto.

2

Table #8

Splinters of thought seem indecent. His gaze
Stitched onto her dress. He finishes breakfast.
Feeling comfortably fascinated.

3

When the dead forsake our dreams
The living must suffice

MATRYOSHKAS

for V. Peppard

I'm alone. The porch. Empty.
Except for a wooden ashtray.
Still. She's there. My neighbor.
Cancerous. Rotting. I watch.
Her. By the chain-linked fence.
In her wheelchair. Staring at.
The street between us. Awash.
In the light of Russian winters.
Do not talk to me about the moon.
She says. Again. *I have not wasted*
My life. I turn the ashtray. Over-
Flowing. Not with the usual cut
Stems. But small flower heads
Of the most delicate white flesh.

LATE DECEMBER

Clearly. Nothing much is happening. Kids continue to wish.
For snow. The rest. For something other than the possible.
Something other than the fog. Settling as thorns. Frozen.
On fences. Winter, in its subtlest arrival, barbs our barriers.
Still. No one misses the ordinary. Not even the blackbirds.
Just as no one, on either side, misses the end of the world.

NOTES

THÉÂTRE DU GRAND GUIGNOL

The title refers to the notorious Parisian shock theatre founded in 1897 by Oscar Méténier, the naturalist playwright. It closed in 1962.

THE OLDEST HANDS IN THE WORLD

"Roman Blonde" is a historical reference to prostitution in Ancient Rome. Required by law—and, some argue, inspired by various depictions of a blonde Venus—Roman prostitutes dyed their hair blonde.

SPADAFORA and CONVERSATIONS NEAR SAN PIERO PATTI, SICILY

Both Spadafora and San Piero Patti are towns in northeastern Sicily.

LA HORA CERO: ESCHATOLOGICAL FRAGMENTS

"*La Hora Cero*" is taken from Astor Piazzolla's last album, *Tango: Zero Hour* (1986). The title refers to Piazzolla's notion of the time after midnight, "an hour of absolute end and absolute beginning," while the line "*tango, tragedia, comedia, kilombo* (whorehouse)" is his formula for the *Nuevo Tango*.

TIME

Inspired by Alan Lightman's *Einstein's Dreams*, a novel.

DOPPELGÄNGER

"*There is no absence that cannot be replaced*" is a line from René Char's poem "Chaîne."

WOOD OF SUICIDES

In Dante's *Inferno*, the "river Phlegethon" serves as the first ring, while the "Wood of Suicides" serves as the second ring, of the seventh circle of hell.

4:36 AM

"*Le Pont Mirabeau*" refers to Guillaume Apollinaire's poem and the place Paul Celan committed suicide.

ACKNOWLEDGMENTS

Grateful recognition is made to these literary periodicals and newspapers, in which many of these poems, sometimes in earlier versions, first appeared: *Absinthe: New European Writing*; *Aperture*; *The Aroostook Review*; *The Baltimore Review*; *The Binturong Review* (U.K.); *Cantilevers*; *Clean Sheets*; *The Cortland Review*; *Erased, Sigh, Sigh*; *Ecloga* (U.K.); *Erbacce* (U.K.); *Fieralingue* (Italy); *Gradiva: International Journal of Italian Poetry* (U.S. and Italy); *Härter* (Germany); *International Poetry* (India); *Italian Americana*; *Jacket* (Australia); *The Ledger, Lilliput Review*; *M.A.G.*; *The Mailer Review*; *Niederngasse* (Switzerland); *Pages* (U.K.); *The Pedestal Magazine*; *Poetenladen* (Germany); *The Toronto Quarterly* (Canada); *The White Whale Review*; and *32 Poems Magazine*.

A number of these poems also appeared in a chapbook: *Panta Rhei* (Alpha Beat Press, New Hope, PA, 2000).

Some of these poems have appeared in the following anthologies: *The Book of Hopes and Dreams* (Bluechrome Press, 2006) (U.K.), *Liverpool Poets 08* (Erbacce Press, 2008) (U.K.), *Poetic Voices Without Borders* (Gival Press, 2005), *Poetic Voices Without Borders 2* (Gival Press, 2009), *Sunscripts* (Florida Center for Writers, 2004 and 2005), and *The Other Voices International Project* (Other Voices Poetry, 2007).

***

The author wishes to thank his wonderful editors at Black Lawrence Press, Colleen Ryor and Diane Goettel, and the English Departments at the University of South Florida, Florida

Southern College, and Edge Hill University. And Matthew Lewis for the "exception." For their valued criticism and lasting friendship, the author is inexpressively grateful to Billy Collins, Jay Hopler, Anthony Lee, Peter Meinke, Gregory Smith, and Victor Peppard. Endless gratitude to James Reidel and Nicholas Samaras for their friendship, inspiration, and guidance. Last, and most important, the author wishes to thank his family for their unceasing love, support, and encouragement.

Daniele Pantano is a Swiss poet, translator, critic, and editor born of Sicilian and German parentage in Langenthal (Canton of Berne). Pantano has taught at the University of South Florida and served as the Visiting Poet-in-Residence at Florida Southern College. He divides his time between Switzerland, the United States, and England, where he's Senior Lecturer in Creative Writing at Edge Hill University. For more information, please visit www.danielepantano.ch.